3x3eyes

サザン　アイズ

...e of Demons

3x3 eyes
サザン アイズ

House of Demons ™

Story and art
YUZO TAKADA

Translation
TOREN SMITH AND
TOSHIFUMI YOSHIDA

Lettering and retouch
WAYNE TRUMAN

Introduction
ROB ZOMBIE

Original series editor
GEORGE BRODERICK, JR.

Collection editor
PEET JANES

Collection design
CARY GRAZZINI

Logo design
MARK COX

DARK HORSE COMICS

MIKE RICHARDSON publisher
NEIL HANKERSON executive vice president
DAVID SCROGGY vice president of publishing
LOU BANK vice president of sales & marketing
ANDY KARABATSOS vice president of finance
MARK ANDERSON general counsel
RANDY STRADLEY creative director
CINDY MARKS director of production & design
MARK COX art director
SEAN TIERNEY computer graphics director
MICHAEL MARTENS director of sales
TOD BORLESKE director of licensing
MARK ELLINGTON director of operations
DALE LAFOUNTAIN director of m.i.s.

Published by Dark Horse Comics
10956 SE Main Street
Milwaukie, OR 97222

ISBN: 1-56971-059-7
First edition: March 1995

10 9 8 7 6 5 4 3 2

Printed in Canada

ATTENTION FANBOY GEEKS—
→ THIS BOOK DOES NOT CONTAIN
MUSCLE-BOUND STEROID FREAKS!!
→ THIS BOOK DOES NOT CONTAIN
SILICONE-PACKING MUTANT BIMBOS
SPORTING DAY-GLO PANTYHOSE!!
→ THIS BOOK DOES CONTAIN
A NUTTY THREE-EYED GIRL NAMED PAT
AND YAKUMO A PSEUDO-TRANSVESTITE
WILDMAN. TOGETHER THEY JOIN
FORCES FOR SOME KOO-KOO
ADVENTURES JACK! SO TURN
OFF YOUR BRAIN KICK BACK IN
AN E-Z CHAIR AND START
SWINGING KIDDIES!

ROB ZOMBIE
9/14/94

CHAPTER ONE:
REBIRTH

PLEASE
Take me to
Junin-Machi in
Shinjuku

WHAT'S WITH THAT GIRL...? JEEZ, SHE'S SURE DIRTY!

JUNIN-MACHI... THAT'S WHERE I LIVE...

. . . .

GUESS I COULD TELL HER HOW TO GET THERE... WHA-?!

WHUD

啊～～～～ッ!!

〈HEY!!〉

〈STOP THIEF!!〉
小偷!!

!!

HEY, YOU!! STO--

STAY OUTTA IT, PUNK!!

WHROK

HRRK!!

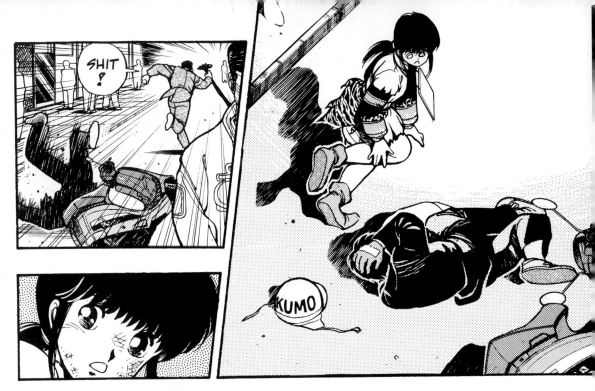

SHIT!?

KUMO

ARE...

ARE YOU OKAY?!

YEAH... OWW...

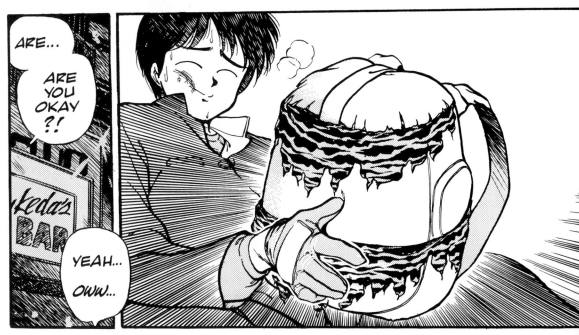

謝謝 シェシェ

THANK YOU SO MUCH!!

HEH, HEH... NO PROB.

SAY... ARE YOU CHINESE? WHAT'S YOUR NAME?

I AM PAI.

NICE NAME! I'M... ER... ....

UMM... LOOK...

I GOTTA TELL YOU...

I'M NOT REALLY A TRANSVESTITE.

?

I COULD NEVER AFFORD TO PAY FOR FOOD AND RENT ON AN ORDINARY PART-TIME JOB.

BESIDES, THEY'D THROW ME OUT OF SCHOOL IF THEY KNEW I WAS WORKING.

WHEN I WAS JUST NINE, MY MOM RAN AWAY FROM HOME. FOUR YEARS LATER, MY DAD WENT MISSING IN TIBET WHILE ON A SCIENTIFIC EXPEDITION.

BUT IF ANY OF MY TEACHERS SEES ME HERE, THEY'RE NOT GONNA SAY ANYTHING, RIGHT?

AND IT PAYS $30 AN HOUR, JUST FOR SERVING DRINKS!

YOU SAY YOU JUST SERVE DRINK, YES? REALLY SO?

EH HEH HEH...

I WONDER HOW WELL SHE UNDERSTANDS JAPANESE...?

HEY, YAKUMO... WHO'S THE SWEETIE?

YEAH, IS SHE YOUR GIRLFRIEND? YOU'RE BREAKING MY HEART!

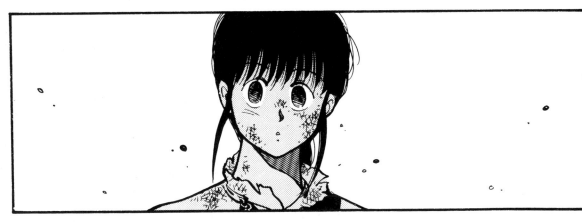

HERE WE THOUGHT YOU WERE SO INNOCENT... SEVENTEEN AND STILL A VIRGIN!

AW, YOU GUYS! C'MON, CUT IT OUT!

YA... KU... MO?

HUH?

WAAH!
YAKUMO!!

FOUR YEARS! I LOOK FOUR YEARS SINCE I LEAVE TIBET!!

OH, YAKUMO!! YAKUMO!!

I...I LOOK SO HARD!

FINALLY I FIND YOU!!

WHA... WHAT THE HELL...?

snff snff

ALL RIGHT, JERK! WHAT DID YOU DO TO THAT POOR GIRL?!

BOSS, YOU GOTTA HELP ME!!

I REALLY DON'T SEE WHY I SHOULD...WELL, WHY DON'T YOU TELL ME WHAT GOT STOLEN. I'LL HAVE A COUPLE OF THE BOYS* LOOK FOR THE MUGGER.

*: YAKUZA (JAPANESE MAFIA) "SOLDIERS"

"I MANAGED TO GRAB HER BACKPACK, BUT HE GOT THIS WEIRD STAFF THING SHE HAD..."

DAMN... ALL THAT, AND THIS IS ALL I GET...

!?!

HUH?

WHAT TH--

AIEE!!

FWHOOSH

TH'K

THIS PROFESSOR FUJII...

MY... MY FATHER...?

snff

HEH HEH...

FOR ME, AS A KID, "PROFESSOR OF ANTHROPOLOGY" JUST MEANT THIS MONSTER-CRAZY OLD GUY WHO LEFT ME AND MY MOM ALONE WHILE HE RAN OFF AROUND THE WORLD CHASING AFTER DREAMS.

COME ON, DEAR-- I THINK YOU NEED A SHOWER.

GEE...I DIDN'T KNOW YOUR DAD WAS AN IMPORTANT SCIENTIST...

"Dear Yakumo: How are you? I hope you have been well..."

"Please forgive your father for not contacting you these past six months..."

"SIX MONTHS"...? IT'S BEEN FOUR YEARS!

"I've been trying to make it overland to Kunmin from Tibet..."

"...but unfortunately, it seems I may be leaving this world right here."

"...Pai is the sole survivor of a mystic race, once said to possess the power of eternal life. I have searched all my life to find this race...

"...the Sanji-yanunkara, the fabled Triclops."

"They've taken a different path in their evolution than man...

"...perhaps you could even call them *monsters.*"

THIS IS **NUTS** !

I'M SO SICK OF THIS LOONEY "MONSTER" OBSESSION OF HIS...!

HEH HEH...

"Pai does not yet know how to use the power of immortality, but she claims to have been alive for the last three hundred years."

PROFESSOR...

"Why did all the others of her race disappear, leaving her behind?"

I WANT BECOME **HUMAN** !!

"It's true...long ago for some unknown reason, they conceived a desire to become human.

VERY WELL, PAI -- I PROMISE TO HELP YOU!

YA-HOO!

"Once they discovered how to do so, they traded their immortality for the brief span of a human."

EVEN IF I DIE... MY SON *YAKUMO* WILL SEE THAT YOUR WISH IS GRANTED.

.....

"Instructions on how to transform a Triclops into a human can be obtained from a specialist named *Aguri* at the *Yogekisha* company in Hong Kong."

...

BAM

"Please, my son! Take Pai to Hong Kong to see Aguri...

it is my last request..."

YOU'VE GOT TO BE *JOKING!* YOU REALLY EXPECT ME TO DROP EVERYTHING AND TAKE THAT GRUBBY--

FATHER... YOU HAVE NO IDEA WHAT MY LIFE HAS BEEN LIKE...

FUJI TV 10
HEADLINE
NEWS

I THOUGHT I MIGHT AS WELL FIX HER UP WITH SOME CLOTHES AND MAKEUP WHILE I WAS AT IT... HEE, HEE!

HOW... HOW I LOOK, YAKUMO?

YOU'RE... YOU'RE *BEAUTIFUL*...

I... UH... I MEAN

"Please fulfill my promise to Pai, Yakumo..."

...

LOOK, IT'S JUST *TOO MUCH* TO ASK! BESIDES, THERE'S NO SUCH THING AS MONSTERS...

<TAKUMI!!>

WHA--?

--AND THE GUNS OF THE POLICE SEEM TO HAVE NO EFFECT. SINCE THIS MONSTROUS CREATURE APPEARED JUST A FEW MINUTES AGO, HUNDREDS HAVE FLED SHINJUKU.

AS YOU CAN SEE, IT APPEARS TO BE SOME SORT OF GIGANTIC MAN-FACED BIRD, A CREATURE OUT OF LEGEND. AUTHORITIES ARE--

HEY! HEY, PAI!!

V/VBAK CULTURE SHOCK

〈ジュヒ〉
橐棐巴
〈タクヒ〉

WAIT UP! WHAT'S THIS "TAKUHI"...?

MY FRIEND!

FROM INSIDE MY STAFF! MY FRIEND!!

WHAT?!

HOLD ON A SEC-- I DON'T WANNA MEET THAT THING!!

<TAKUHI, *STOP!!* DON'T YOU RECOGNIZE ME?!>

KREEAA!!

THE MONSTER'S GETTING OUT OF CONTROL!!

UNFORTUNATELY, THE LATEST REPORTS ARE THAT THE NATIONAL GUARD HAS NOT YET BEEN MOBILIZED!

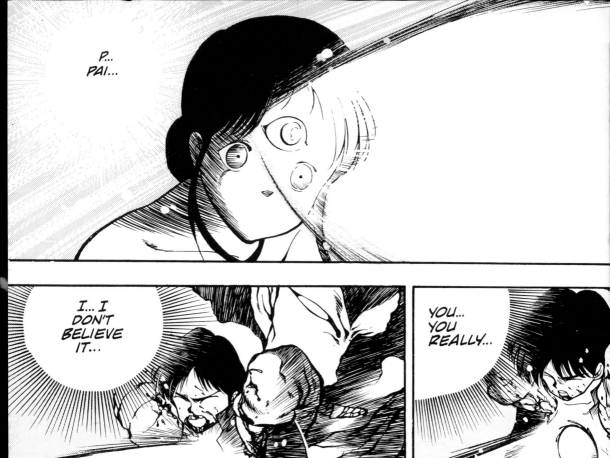

P... PAI...

I... I DON'T BELIEVE IT...

YOU... YOU REALLY...

...AREN'T HUMAN...

SSSs HHHH

YAKUMO...

IN THIS HARSH LIGHT OF DAWN, LAST NIGHT SEEMS LIKE A DREAM.

WHERE DID THAT MONSTER BIRD COME FROM? WHERE DID IT DISAPPEAR TO?

AND FURTHERMORE...

...WHAT WAS THAT EERIE LIGHT THAT ENVELOPED THE GIANT CREATURE?

SO MANY MYSTERIES...

...

THERE'S NO BLOOD...? AND THERE'S PAI'S STAFF!

IT...IT WASN'T JUST A DREAM, WAS IT...?

. . . . .

YA... YAKUMO...

Chapter Two:

Sanjiyan

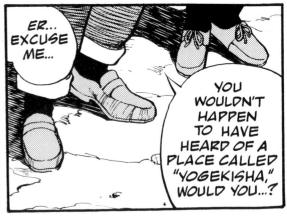

ER... EXCUSE ME...

YOU WOULDN'T HAPPEN TO HAVE HEARD OF A PLACE CALLED "YOGEKISHA," WOULD YOU...?

THIS IS PAI...WE CAME ALL THE WAY TO HONG KONG TO GET SOME INFORMATION ON TURNING A TRICLODS...ER, A KIND OF MONSTER... INTO A HUMAN, AT THIS YOGEKISHA PLACE.

HEH, HEH... Y'KNOW, I DON'T THINK YOU GUYS CAN UNDERSTAND A WORD OF JAPANESE...

ALL RIGHT, PAI...YOUR TURN. *YOU* TALK TO THEM!

SURE!

wheww

THEY GOING TO MAKE ME **HUMAN**-- THAT **GREAT,** YES?

HEE HEE HEE

・・・・・

ACK!

HEY...

I WAS WONDERING...

...JUST WHY IS IT THAT YOU WANT TO BECOME HUMAN?

DON'T KNOW!

I BEEN WANTING IT FOR *300* YEARS...

...BUT I FORGOTTEN WHY!

HUH ?!

PAI... ?

OW OW OW...

!?

DAMN, THAT HURT! AND MY PANTS ARE WRECKED!

LEARN HOW TO DRIVE, MAC! DON'T YOU KNOW WHAT A **WALK** SIGNAL LOOKS LIKE?

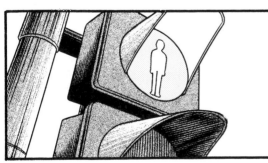

ER...

...OOPS!

S-SORRY ABOUT THAT!!

WHAT HAPPEN, YAKUMO?! YOU HURT YOUR KNEE?!

I THOUGHT I DID, BUT...

<HEY...>

<HEY, KID-- ARE YOU REALLY ALL RIGHT?>

HUH?

<I SAW YOU GET RUN OVER BY THAT BUS!>

UH, NO, I...

<I CAN NOT SPEAK CHINESE.>

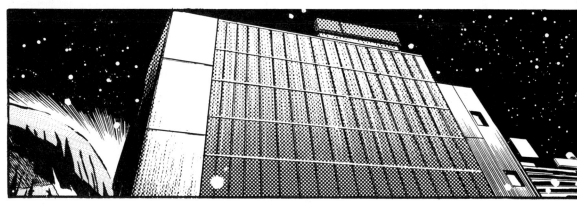

THIS IS ALL REALLY WEIRD.

WHENEVER I GET HURT IT HEALS UP REAL FAST...

...EVER SINCE TAKUHI ALMOST KILLED ME...

...AND THIS MARK APPEARED ON MY FOREHEAD.

WHAT'S HAPPENED TO ME...?

SKSSSHHH

.....

KCHAK

GUESS ALL I CAN DO IS FIND YOGEKISHA AS SOON AS POSSIBLE, AND ASK THEM ABOUT THIS, TOO.

.....

MAN, NOTHING FAZES HER!

ZZZZZ

THIS IS A WASTE OF TIME-- WE NEED MORE INFO.

SURE HOPE WE STUMBLE ACROSS SOMETHING IN THE NEXT TWO DAYS...*

. . . .

SORRY TO BE SO MUCH TROUBLE...

AW, FORGET IT! IT'S NO PROBLEM, REALLY!

YOU KNEE IS HURT, SO PLEASE GO BACK TO HOTEL AND REST, OKAY?

H-HEY! WAIT--

*: A 2 NIGHT/3 DAY HONG KONG TRIP FROM TOKYO COSTS ABOUT $600 PER PERSON.

IT OKAY! I CAN LOOK BY MYSELF OKAY! BYE-BYE! ♥

WAIT! DON'T LEAVE ME ALONE HERE! MY KNEE'S PERFECT ALREADY!

I CAN'T SPEAK CHINESE! PAI!

WHMP

OOPS! S-SORRY!

DAMN...

AFTER HAVING WALKED ALL THE WAY FROM TIBET, SHE'S REALLY *FAST!*

GEEZ, I DON'T EVEN KNOW HOW TO GET BACK TO MY HOTEL!

WITH ONLY TWO MORE DAYS, I CAN'T WASTE TIME JUST SITTING AROUND...

WELL, NOW WHAT?

IN TOKYO I COULD JUST ASK AT A POLICE STATION...

THAT *IT!!* THE POLICE! THE COPS OUGHTA BE ABLE TO FIND OUT WHERE YOGEKISHA IS!

. . . . .

RIGHT! I'LL TAKE A TAXI!

!!

TAXI

MY...

MY WALLET...

SO HOW DO I FIND A POLICE STATION...?

KANG

DAMN IT!!

WARNING
BEWARE OF PICKPOCKETS

NOW YOU TELL ME!!

WHY DOES THIS STUFF ALWAYS HAPPEN TO ME?!

KRRASHANGG

.....

<EXCUSE ME, SIR...
I'M AFRAID YOU'LL
HAVE TO COME
TO THE STATION
WITH US...>

.....

<WE HAVE A JAPANESE
BOY IN CUSTODY
WHO CLAIMS TO BE
LOOKING FOR A MR.
AGURI AT YOUR
COMPANY. CAN WE
LEAVE HIM WITH YOU?>

YUGEKISHA

<MR. AGURI IS AWAY
AT PRESENT...
I'D RATHER NOT
HAVE ANY TROUBLE...>

妖撃社
YOGEKISHA

<HEY!! IT'S
THAT
INVINCIBLE
KID FROM
YESTERDAY!!>

Huh
?

MR. AGURI IS THE CHIEF EDITOR, BUT HE'S NOT IN JUST NOW.

I'M THE ASSISTANT EDITOR, LI LING-LING. SORRY, MY JAPANESE IS A LITTLE RUSTY...

THAT'S OKAY... GEE, I DIDN'T KNOW THAT YOGEKISHA WAS A PUBLISHING COMPANY...

WE'VE BEEN PUBLISHING OCCULT MAGAZINES AND BOOKS SINCE LONG BEFORE THE "GHOSTBUSTERS" BOOM, EVEN THOUGH OUR SALES WERE ONLY SO-SO.

WE COVER THE USUAL SORT OF STUFF... GHOSTS, POLTERGEISTS, MONSTERS... YOU KNOW. NOTHING TOO FANCY.

LET'S SEE...

WHUD

YOU WANTED TO KNOW ABOUT THE *TRICLOPS*... WE CALL THEM THE "*SANJIYAN*"...

"SANJIYAN UNKARA... BEAUTIFUL IN APPEARANCE, AN IMMORTAL THREE-EYED CREATURE..."

"...OFTEN BEWITCHING THE HUMAN HEART. ONCE IN THEIR LIFE THEY DEVOUR A HUMAN SOUL."

!!

...UMM... "FURTHERMORE..."

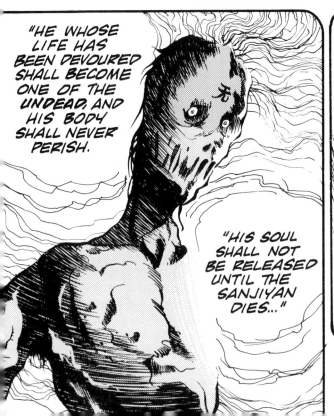

"HE WHOSE LIFE HAS BEEN DEVOURED SHALL BECOME ONE OF THE UNDEAD, AND HIS BODY SHALL NEVER PERISH.

"HIS SOUL SHALL NOT BE RELEASED UNTIL THE SANJIYAN DIES..."

"AND UPON HE WHOSE SOUL HAS BEEN DEVOURED SHALL APPEAR THE SYMBOL '无.'"

无

"无" MEANS "NOTHINGNESS," OR "THE VOID"

YAKUMO!

I REALLY GLAD TO SEE YOU!! ♥

I SO WORRIED WHEN I FIND YOU NOT HERE!

WHERE HAVE YOU BEEN?

YOU HUNGRY? LET'S GO EAT!

UNTIL THEN... ...BE THANKFUL FOR THIS IMMORTAL BODY I HAVE GIVEN YOU!!

"I UNDERSTAND NOW, PAI..."

"YOU SAVED MY LIFE..."

"I'D FORGOTTEN ALL ABOUT MY PROMISE TO MAKE YOU HUMAN..."

"WHAT A FOOL I'VE BEEN!"

"BUT..."

"HOW CAN I DO IT? HOW CAN I MAKE YOU HUMAN...?"

302

NOK NOK

H... HELLO?

EXCUSE ME... ISN'T THIS YAKUMO FUJII'S ROOM? WHAT HAPPENED TO THE WINDOW?

WHERE'S YAKUMO?

I... I DON'T KNOW. IT WAS LIKE THIS WHEN I WOKE UP... I DON'T REMEMBER WHAT HAPPENED. WHO ARE YOU?

MY NAME IS LI LING-LING, FROM YOGEKISHA.

I'VE COME HERE TO GIVE YAKUMO SOME INFORMATION ON THE TRANSFORMATION OF A TRICLOPS TO A HUMAN.

LOOKING THROUGH MR. AGURI'S SECRET FILES, I CAME ACROSS THIS PHOTO...

TOP SECRET

LET... LET ME SEE IT!?

OH, NO, YOU DON'T! LET'S MAKE A DEAL-- YOU TELL ME THE SECRET OF YAKUMO'S INVULNERABILITY, AND THEN I'LL SHOW YOU THE PHOTO!

OK, OK...

GO AHEAD...I FOUND IT IN A FILE MARKED "HUMANIFI-CATION." I HAVE NO IDEA WHAT IT IS OR WHAT IT MEANS...

THIS...

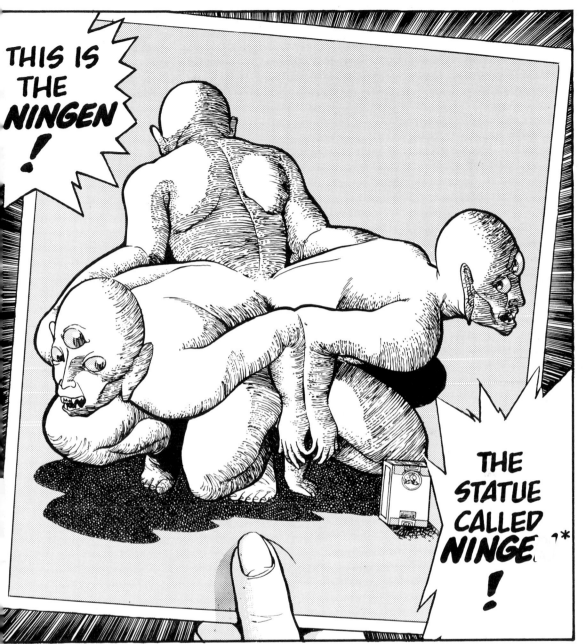

*: MEANS "HUMANITY"

THIS MUST BE IT...

MY GOD!! THE **NINGEN!!**

K-GHAK

WHA--?!

!!

DAMN IT!!

SEIZ
HIM

OH, MAN!!

I'M IN TROUBLE NOW!!

HALT!!

!!

TH-THIS IS NO FAKE CULT!!

THEY WORSHIP THE *TRICLOPS GOD!* AND--

--THEY'RE NOT EVEN HUMAN!!

NO!

PLEASE...

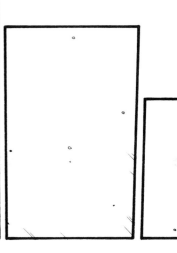

LADY HUANG, STOP!

WE NEED TO FIND OUT HOW MUCH HE KNOWS, OR IF HE'S WORKING WITH ANYONE ELSE!

TOO LATE...

IT IS DONE!

YOU READY FOR LUNCH, YAKUMO...?

YOU BET!!

WHAT ARE YOU DOING?

HOMEWORK... I'M SUPPOSED TO FINISH THIS DURING WINTER BREAK.

BREAK'S OVER IN A COUPLE WEEKS AND I'VE BARELY STARTED... HEH, HEH... IT'S NOT GOING VERY WELL, EITHER...

....

ALL HIS ANSWERS ARE WRONG...

WOW! LOOKS DELICIOUS!

CALCULUS II

GEE, YOU GUYS ARE SURE BEING NICE... LETTING US STAY HERE AND ALL... WE REALLY OWE YOU ONE!

HEH HEH

SMAK

WELL... I HAVE MY REASONS...

PAI! TIME FOR LUNCH!

YOU SEE... HEH, HEH... I'VE FIGURED IT OUT.

....Hmph!!

THE LEAST YOU COULD DO IS LISTEN TO ME!!

YOU'RE A **NINJA**, RIGHT? YOU WEREN'T EVEN SCRATCHED WHEN THE BUS HIT YOU! SO, I THINK YOU OUGHT TO BE WORTH A FEATURE ARTICLE, ANYWAY...

HEY, PAI!

I WONDER WHAT'S WRONG WITH HER...

SHE'S BEEN ACTING STRANGE EVER SINCE SHE SAW THAT STATUE...

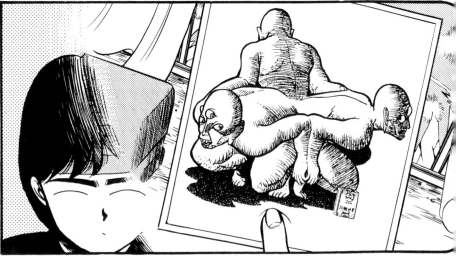

THE NINGEN...

"LONG AGO, WHEN I WAS A CHILD, I VAGUELY REMEMBER HAVING SEEN THIS STATUE."

"EVENTS OF THREE HUNDRED YEARS AGO, THAT I HAVEN'T BEEN ABLE TO RECALL UNTIL NOW..."

"I CAN'T REMEMBER ANYTHING ELSE...

WHY...?"

WHAT'S THE MATTER, PAI?

YOU SEEM A LITTLE DOWN...

PAI ALWAYS IN A GOOD MOOD!

AW, YAKUMO...♪

SOMETHING IS WRONG-- THAT'S NOT HER NORMAL SMILE!

GRRGGLE

HUNGRY, HUH? LOOK AT THE GREAT LUNCH LING LING GOT US!!

WOW!

LOOKS DELICIOUS!

PAI IS HUNGRY! ESPECIALLY FOR *HUMAN* FOOD!

SAY... SINCE LING LING GOT FOOD FOR US, WE SHOULD SHARE WITH HER, YES?

BUT...

IT WILL TASTE BETTER IF WE SHARE!

WOMEN... UH, I MEAN *MONSTERS*... WHO CAN UNDERSTAND THEM...?

YOGEKISHA

?

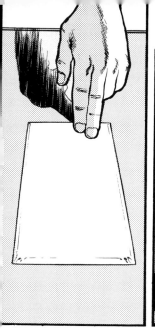

PLEASE...I BEG OF YOU!

....

VERY WELL, THEN-- WE ACCEPT.

PLEASE WAIT IN YOUR CAR WHILE WE PREPARE.

WHO WAS THAT...?

HEE HEE

HE WANTS TO HIRE OUR COMPANY!

HIS BOSS IS ONE OF THE RICHEST MEN IN HONG KONG... AND HE SAYS HE'S HAUNTED BY DEMONS.

妖撃社
YOGEKISHA

DEMONS...? NOT TRICLOPS?!

...

LOOK, YAKUMO...

WE BOTH KNOW MONSTERS AND DEMONS DON'T REALLY EXIST...

BUT WORK IS WORK!!

I MAY NOT BELIEVE IN MONSTERS, BUT I SURE BELIEVE IN MONEY!!

WE DON'T EXIST...?

AND FOR 45,000 HONG KONG DOLLARS*, I'LL BELIEVE IN WHATEVER THEY WANT!

*: ABOUT $6,000 U.S

WAIT A SEC... IF THOSE TWO ARE NINJAS OR SOMETHING, THEY COULD COME IN HANDY.

HMM...

WE'LL STAY HERE...

SAY...WHY DON'T YOU TWO COME ALONG AS MY ASSISTANTS? THEY'VE GOT BUCK-ETS OF MONEY, SO AT LEAST THE FOOD OUGHT TO BE PRETTY GOOD...

I'M GOING!! PAI'S GOING!! ♡

.....

WELCOME TO MY HOME, EVERYONE-- MY APOLOGIES FOR THE DELAY.

I AM THE MASTER OF THIS HOUSE, HUANG SONG LI.

PLEASED TO MEET YOU-- I AM LI LING LING OF YOGEKISHA... THESE ARE MY ASSISTANTS.

LET'S GET RIGHT TO THE POINT-- WHAT EXACTLY HAS HAPPENED HERE?

YAY!

SHH! YOU GOTTA TRANSLATE FOR ME!

IT WAS ABOUT ONE MONTH AGO...

"...WHILE IT POURED RAIN..."

SKRKK

?!

"I WAS AWAKENED BY THE SOUND OF SOMETHING BEING TORN APART..."

SHRAK

"THEN I NOTICED THAT I WAS DRESSED IN SOME OUTRAGEOUS COSTUME..."

!!

"...AND I HAD NO IDEA HOW I CAME TO BE WEARING IT!"

DARLING! WHERE ARE YOU?!

"I THOUGHT IT WAS ONE OF MY HUSBAND'S JOKES, SO I HEADED FOR HIS STUDY..."

REALLY, DEAR, THIS IS NOT--

D-DEAR...

RLING!!

barf...

ULP!

POOR GUY...

SO I'VE LOST MY HUSBAND...AND THOSE THREE-CLAW MARKS ARE MADE EVERY NIGHT HERE IN THE MANSION...

I AWAKEN WEARING STRANGE CLOTHING...

PLEASE... YOU MUST HELP ME! IF THIS GOES ON, I FEAR I WILL GO INSANE...

I FEEL SORRY FOR HER, BUT...

...WE'VE GOT OUR OWN PROBLEMS TO THINK ABOUT!

IF AGURI CALLS WHILE WE'RE HERE, WE'LL MISS IT. AND I'VE GOT SCHOOL AND MY JOB IN JAPAN...

RIGHT, PAI...?

LOOKS LIKE SHE'S DEPRESSED AGAIN... THINKING ABOUT THAT STATUE, I'LL BET...

HEY, HEY... CHEER UP!

IF IT'S THAT *NINGEN* STATUE YOU'RE SO WORRIED ABOUT, I'LL GET IT FOR YOU, NEVER FEAR!

HEH, HEH!

DON'T WORRY ABOUT ME... I--

SKRAK!

EEEK!

PAI! ARE YOU OKAY?!

YES... THIS WOOD JUST ROTTEN...

I SORRY, YAKUMO... IT JUST THAT WHEN I SEE THAT PICTURE, THE PAST COME BACK TO ME...

I WAS WITH MY PEOPLE THEN...

AND... AND NOW... I ALL ALONE...

~sniff~

FWAK

Y-YOU'RE NOT ALONE...

PAI...

I... I...

I... I...

I...

I...

?

I'LL ALWAYS BE WITH YOU!

?!

N... NO!!

WHEW...

TOO CLOSE FOR MY TASTE...

TH- THIS SOME KIND OF JOKE...?

SORRY I WORRY YOU, YAKUMO...

I'VE BEEN ACTING STRANGE, IT TRUE...

BUT PAI'S GOT YOU NOW... AND SO I VERY VERY HAPPY...

....

HEH...

MS. HUANG!

I F-FOUND HER LIKE THIS WHILE I WAS SEARCHING THE M-M-MANSION...

IT'S OKAY, YAKUMO...

SHE STILL ALIVE! HELP ME!

GOT IT!

WHAT'S GOING ON HERE?

WHAT ARE YOU DOING IN THE MASTER'S STUDY?!

MADAME!

A HIDDEN SAFE...?

THAT'S STRANGE.

WHATEVER IT WAS, IT SURE WANTED INTO THAT SAFE...

WHAT THIS?

OOPS... SORRY ABOUT THAT...

VREEEE

KLIK

AS YOU CAN SEE, THIS IS FOOTAGE TAKEN BY THE HIDDEN CAMERA I SET UP IN THE CEILING. AFTERWARDS, THE "CLAW" CONTINUES TO SCRATCH AT THE SAFE.

....

....

MR. CHOU, JUST **WHAT** IS INSIDE OF THAT SAFE...?

COULD IT BE THAT THE "CLAW" IS AFTER WHATEVER IT IS INSIDE?

.....

TH...THAT MAY BE SO.

‹YOU SHOULD BE IN BED!›

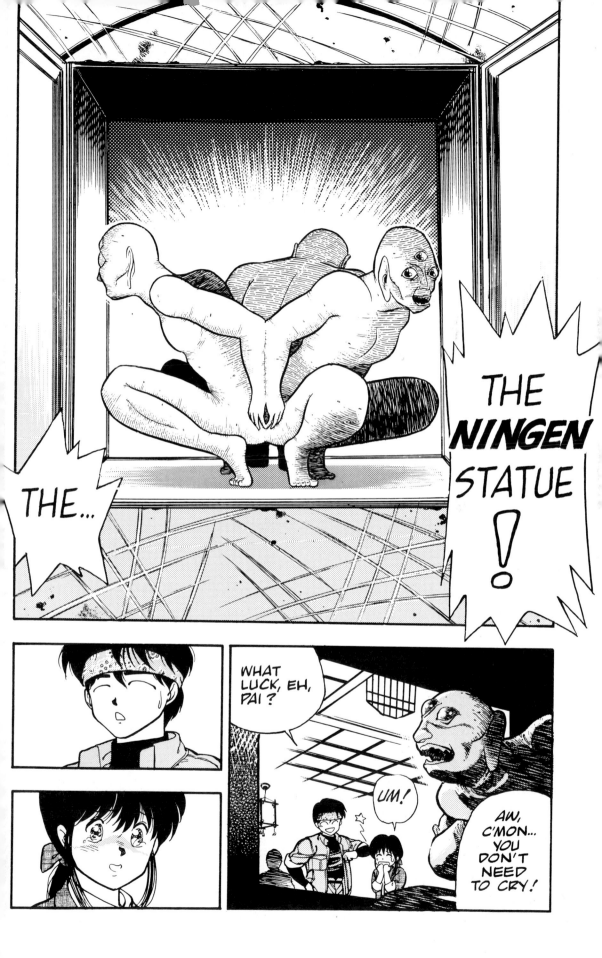

HEY!!

REALLY, CHOU, I SEE NO HARM IN LETTING THEM EXAMINE THE STATUE.

NO, MADAME-- WE MUSTN'T.

WHAT WOULD WE HAVE TO DO IN ORDER FO YOU TO TRUS US?

OH, I DON'T KNOW... PERHAPS IF YOU DEFEATED THE THREE-CLAWED DEMON, WE COULD LOAN THE STATUE TO YOU.

WE'LL DO IT!

I'M GONNA REGRET THIS...

ER...OF COURSE, WE WON'T DO IT FOR *NOTHING!* IT'LL COST YOU... AH...HK$3000 A DAY, PLUS EXPENSES.

AND, IF YOU ACT NOW...

WHOOSH

...WE'LL INCLUDE THESE WARDS THAT KEEP AWAY MONSTERS FOR THE LOW, LOW PRICE OF ONLY HK$750 EACH!

URK!

GULP!

JUST PLACE THIS ON YOUR SAFE...

...AND MONSTERS WILL BE UNABLE TO TOUCH IT!

TIME FOR US TO RETIRE, MADAME...

THESE ELEGANT WARDS WERE CRAFTED BY A WELL-KNOWN AND POWERFUL TAOIST MONK! THEY ALSO COME IN A ECONOMICAL SET OF TEN, WHICH IS PAYABLE IN TWELVE LOW MONTHLY INSTALLMENTS OF HK$620...

...

=Waaah!= I'M ALL ALONE!

GOOD LUCK, YAKUMO! ♡

THANKS!

OH, WELL...MY FAULT FOR ACTING SO TOUGH.

ANYWAY, WHAT ARE WE GOING TO DO NOW, LING LING?

LET'S SEE...

DON'T MENTION IT. YOU CAN DO ANYTHING WHEN YOU'RE NOT AFRAID TO DIE...

I JUST HAVE TO WORRY ABOUT THAT *WARD*...

CAMERA AND CAMCORDER...

TRACER BUGS AND TRACKING RECEIVER...

NIGHT-SIGHT GOGGLES... SURVIVAL KNIFE...

AND VARIOUS OTHER GOODIES... WE'RE ALL SET!

OKAY... YAKUMO, PAI-- LET'S GO!

MS. HUANG ISN'T GOING TO LIKE IT...

WHAT'S THE MATTER, PAI?

I CAN FEEL IT... THE ONE FROM YESTERDAY IS NEAR...

"THE ONE FROM YESTERDAY"...?

WHA...

WHAT HAPPENED...?

WHY DID IT JUST RUN AWAY?

whewww

SO... WE END UP LOSING THE *NINGEN*, AND STARTING A FIRE...

SOMEHOW, I DON'T THINK MS. HUANG IS GOING TO BE TOO IMPRESSED.

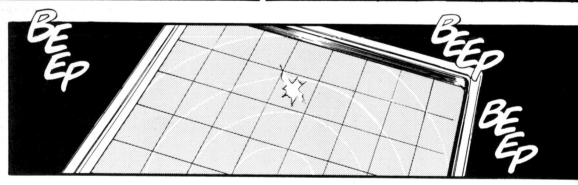

BEEP *BEEP* *BEEP*

HEH HEH! JUST AS I PLANNED... I PLANTED A TRACER ON THAT STATUE...

...AND IT'S STILL IN THE MANSION!

BEEP BEEP BEEP

TO BE CONCLUDED...

YOU'RE **LATE** !!

JUST WHAT WERE YOU TWO DOING ?!

huhh

huhh

SORR !

WE WERE FILLING THE FOUNTAIN IN THE GARDEN WITH GASOLINE.

THE **CLAW MONSTER** SEEMS TO HATE LIGHT, SO WE'RE GOING TO DRIVE IT INTO THE FOUNTAIN WITH THE FLASHLIGHT AND **TORCH** IT !

BEEP

BEEP

BEEP

YEAH...

IF THE STATUE REALLY HOLDS THE SECRET TO MAKE YOU HUMAN...

...IT WON'T BE LONG NOW, PAI.

WHAT DO YOU PLAN TO DO WHEN YOU BECOME HUMAN...?

CAREFUL, THE STAIRS ARE STEEP...

HUH?

$$

MM!

.....

DON'T YOU KNOW?

HEY, YAKUMO!

FOUND IT! IT'S IN HERE!

BEEP BEEP BEEP

HUH?

BTAM!

SKRASSH!

H-HOW DID YOU...?!

SO!! YOU'RE THE THIEF!!

LING LING! DON'T!! YOU'LL GET HURT!!

鈴鈴
!!
<LING LING!!>

HYA!!

I WON'T FALL FOR *THAT* ONE AGAIN!

ENOUGH OF YOUR STUPID TRICKS!

!?

HRRK!

UHH...

TOCHAU* KILL THEM!

*: "EARTH CLAW"

NOT SO FAST, BUDDY!!

DAMN YOU!

LING LING!

!!

THAT'S OKAY AS LONG AS YOU'RE ALL RIGHT.

BUT YAKUMO... IT STILL IN THE ROOM!

IT WAITING FOR US AT THE DOOR...

THAT'S JUST GREAT!! WITHOUT THE LIGHT WE CAN'T EVEN GET AWAY FROM IT, NEVER MIND GET RID OF IT!

YES...

THERE'S GOT TO BE SOME--

HMM?!

SKRAK

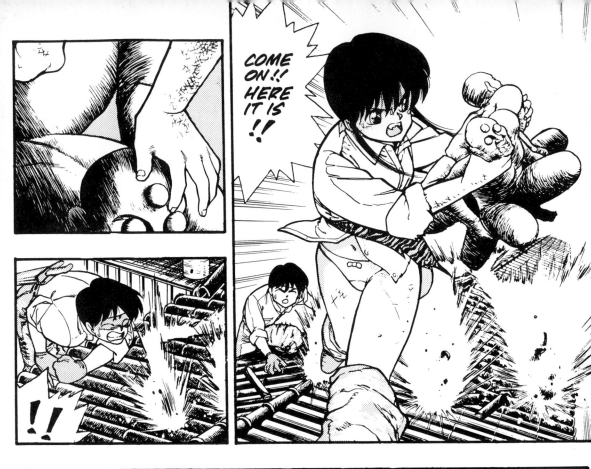

COME ON!! HERE IT IS!!

YOU IDIOT!

WHAT ARE YOU DOING?

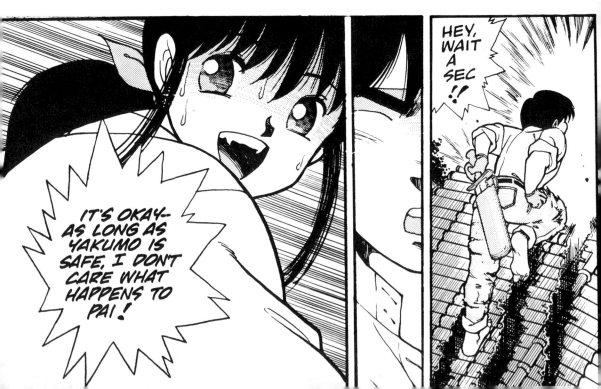

HEY, WAIT A SEC!!

IT'S OKAY— AS LONG AS YAKUMO IS SAFE, I DON'T CARE WHAT HAPPENS TO PAI!

HEH HEH HEH

YOU...

YOU HAVE BETRAYED... HSUNKAI...

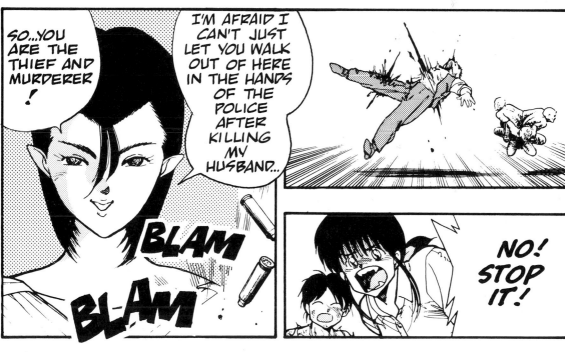

SO...YOU ARE THE THIEF AND MURDERER!

I'M AFRAID I CAN'T JUST LET YOU WALK OUT OF HERE IN THE HANDS OF THE POLICE AFTER KILLING MY HUSBAND...

BLAM

BL-AM

NO! STOP IT!

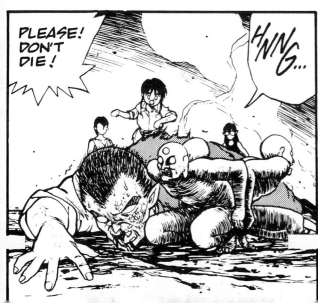

PLEASE! DON'T DIE!

HNNG...

Y-YOU...

Heh.... THE *NINGEN* WILL ONCE AGAIN RETURN UNTO THE WORLD OF DARKNESS...

HSSHH

CHOU, YOU--!!

D-DESPAIR IN YOUR SEARCH...

HNK

GEEZ... TALK ABOUT A WASTE OF TIME...

LOOKS LIKE I'M NOT GOING BACK TO MY OLD LIFE FOR A WHILE, HUH...

BUT...

STILL...

...PAI IS KIND OF *HAPPY*, ANYWAY.

HUH? WHAT ARE YOU SMILING ABOUT?

YOU KNOW!

DON'T YOU REALIZE YOU'RE *ALWAYS* GOING TO BE A DEMON?

FOR A WHILE, YES!

AND "FOR A WHILE" WE'RE GOING TO BE AS ONE, I GUESS!

UH-UH!!

FOR ALWAYS!

WELL, WHATEVER!

I BEG YOUR FORGIVENESS, GREAT *KAIYAN WANG*...

I SWEAR TO RECOVER THE STATUE BEFORE YOUR RETURN...

...AND I BEG YOUR FORGIVENESS.

HOW... INTERESTING...

STILL...

THAT BOY HAS THE MARK OF "无"...

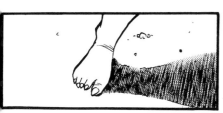

PAI'S REALLY HUNGRY! ♡

AW, COME ON-- TAKE IT EASY-- I GOTTA PAY FOR ALL THIS!

MY POOR WALLET...

END OF **HOUSE OF DEMONS** MINISERIES—
BUT YAKUMO AND PAI WILL BE BACK!